73

DEAR
FUTURE
BOYFRIEND

BY CRISTIN O'KEEFE APTOWICZ

A Write Bloody Book
Long Beach, CA USA

Dear Future Boyfriend
a collection of poetry

ଓ

by Cristin O'Keefe Aptowicz

Write Bloody Publishing
America's Independent Press

Long Beach, CA

writebloody.com

Aptowicz, Cristin O'Keefe.
1ˢᵗ edition.
ISBN: 978-1-935904-70-0

Interior Layout by Lea C. Deschenes
Cover Designed by Joshua Grieve
Proofread by Sarah Kay
Edited by Derrick Brown and Sarah Kay
Author Photo by Alex Brook Lynn
Type set in Helvetica by Linotype and Bergamo (www.theleagueofmoveabletype.com)

Special thanks to Lightning Bolt Donor, Weston Renoud

Printed in Tennessee, USA

Write Bloody Publishing
Long Beach, CA
Support Independent Presses
writebloody.com

To contact the author, send an email to writebloody@gmail.com

DEAR FUTURE BOYFRIEND

MOTHER

When I told my mother
I wanted to be a veterinarian
when I grew up, she told me
that vets kill puppies and kittens
and stick needles into horses
and bunnies with cancer.

When I told my mother
I wanted to be a zoo-keeper
when I grew up, she told me
that animals in captivity
are still wild animals, and hence
could attack even the friendliest
of caretakers, usually tearing them
to shreds and eating their remains.

You see, my mom and I
had a lot of time to talk
about these things: I was the last
of the Aptowicz brood.

Always too young and too small
to go on the backpacking trips
and nature hikes that formed
my brother and sister: the scientists.

No, it was always just Mom and me,
a stack of books, and NPR coming through
the radio like the voice of God.

Mom never liked my career choices much,
but I knew I was on the right track
when one day, over a bowl of alphabet soup,

I asked her:

> Hey Mom,
> how come there are such things
> as bad words?

And she said:

> Honey,
> there is no such thing
> as a "bad word."
> Only words that aren't
> appropriate for all situations.
>
> For instance,
> you should never say
> the word "shit"
> in front of a nun.

You see, she gave me that:
she gave me the gift of words;
she gave me the power of words,
and I never considered it a privilege.

But my mom grew up in a time
when words were being redefined,
words like gender, power, class,
and revolution.

She grew up in a house
where a wrench spray-painted gold
would serve as a shower dial,
and a father overseas would somehow
support a wife and four kids
left stateside, being my mother,
her sister, and two sons
who wouldn't even recognize
their father when he returned home
four years later.

Eating meat once a week,
recycling shoes to the next kid in line,
and using your babysitting money
to buy groceries,

even my mom knew the score.

So though she was top of her class,
editor of the school literary magazine,
editor of the school newspaper,
the National Merit Scholar with
the three-newspapers-a-day habit,
she still had to hear them tell her:

> *The scholarship*
> *is not going to be for English.*
> *If you want to go to college at all,*
> *it's going to have to be for science.*

So my mother, the biologist,
met my father, the chemical engineer,
and together they produced three beautiful kids,
one of which my mom would make sure
wouldn't feel the burn she was forced to feel.

One government paycheck and three kids
under the age of four doesn't go very far,
but Mom always made sure we had books,
even if it meant we rolled pennies
instead of dice, or bought our Christmas
gifts from our neighbor's garage sale.

People always ask me
why I make such a big deal
correcting them, saying:

> *No, it's not*
> *Cristin Aptowicz.*

> *It's Cristin O'Keefe Aptowicz.*

It's just one word, they say,
it shouldn't make that much difference.

But I know the differences words make.
It is a gift my mother gave me.

And I honor her
every time I put pen to paper,
every time I put word to lip,
and every time I sign my name,

because I know
that in order for me
to be who I am,
to live how I live,
to write how I write,

it took
Maureen Anne O'Keefe
the visionary, the writer,

to become
Maureen Aptowicz,
the wife, the mother.

My mother says she'd never trade
any of us kids in for a novel, or
a job at the *New York Times*,
though the way we behave sometimes,
she says she'd consider it.

But I know she's only joking,
because I have never seen her
look so proud, or smile so bright,
as when I finally told her
what I wanted to do,

and she said:

You know what, honey?

I think
Cristin O'Keefe Aptowicz
is the perfect name

for a writer.

FATHER

At the age of one, my friend Ernie
was yanked out of his trailer and
into the air, by no joke, a tornado.

At the age of one, in Ashland, Ohio,
my friend Ernie was swept up into
the kickbox of a tornado,

swung around a bit, and landed
without a single scratch on him
on top of a pile of wood and metal.

He's twenty-five now, and I tell him:
*That's the best fucking bar story
I've ever heard.*

All I lost was a sock, Ernie says,
showing me his worn clipping:
him as a baby, and underneath

that photo, the caption reads:
"All He Lost Was A Sock."
Lots of babies were lost in that storm,

he said, *they had to identify me
with footprints.* At home in Astoria,
there is a storm outside my window,

and I am in front of my computer,
wondering what it'd mean to be him,
to be the one baby found living.

I mean, if that had been me,
would I really be slaving over
another poem about heartbreak?

Every summer my dad would catch
the loud plump bodies of bullfrogs
to teach us kids the compassion of nature,

or maybe the nature of compassion,
tucking the slick cold frogs into our hands,
telling us not to hold too tightly,

making us marvel at the froggy form,
the webbed feet, rounded eyes, bodies
like great green danishes, and then,

after we were done, and sometimes
before, he would tell us to let them go.
We would, always sad, and watch

them hop and jump and slip into water,
finally disappearing as smoothly and
as cleanly as a poem by Basho.

I am home in Astoria, and I am stuck inside.
I call Ernie to talk, ask if he ever thinks
about the tornado and what it means, and

he says, *No, I can't remember it anyway.*
Both his parents have since passed on,
swept up into their own wind.

Life's like that sometimes, he says.
I worry about my father, how he has
started the startling habit of abandoning

the highway when walking, to trek
underneath the bridge to the abandoned
railroad tracks, to keep Zeke, the family dog,

from the speeding grills of trucks.
The dog is just too dumb, Dad says,
and too curious to keep his fat snout

out of the highway, and when you come
to the highway bridge, you don't
have a lot of room to be sniffing.

I try to convince him of other options, but
he won't budge. Dad doesn't want to yank
the dog taunt to the highway shoulder,

nor does he want to awkwardly lift the dog
and stumble across the bridge, nor stop
the walk there, turn around and go home.

No, Dad lets them both take the hard route,
the dark route, underneath the problem,
and sure, it's not the safest idea,

but they are doing it together
and at their own pace, and eventually
they come out the other side alright.

And that's the end of it.
Dad. Father. Catcher of frogs,
there is a storm outside my window,

and I am writing this poem for you.
You, who filled my childhood with amphibians.
You, who fuelled my education with the steady

kinetics of a government paycheck.
You, who walk under bridges to protect
the fat dumb bodies of dogs.

The wind is picking up outside and
the freezing rain is furiously rapping
on my window, sounding like the excited

tappings of a poet who suddenly finds herself
typing a poem she has been trying to write for years.
The wind is picking up outside, Dad,

but I am not afraid, because of you.
I know the compassion of nature and
not just the fat bodies of frogs that you caught,

because more importantly, you caught us,
your children, midrun, and lifted us
into the air, admired us for each

of our intricacies. And when it was time,
and sometimes before, Dad, you let us go
without question, without fear, and we would

disappear away from you into academia,
into New York City, into our own lives
as quick and as seamless as a frog into water.

And you trusted us, trusted us to trust ourselves,
let us walk the harder road if we wanted to,
but we were not alone. You were always

by our side, even if it was too dark to tell,
even when trouble loomed above us
like an easy solution, you never left us

and never questioned us, and you never asked
Why? And if this wall were split by wind
right now, I would let myself be lifted up,

because that is where I feel like going,
outside, into the air, to split this computer
against the sky and let this poem rain down

on all of New York City, to tell them all
about the nature of a father's love,
the inarticulateness of a poet's affections,

and about how 200 miles to Philadelphia
feels like nothing when I think about all
the parts of you still stuck up in me.

And if I fall to the earth, knocked out,
blacked out, and limp, I still will not
be afraid and they will know who I am

without even taking off my socks.
In my family, we would not be identified
by the prints on the soles of our feet.

They would know who we were
by the prints on our back: the size and shape
of our father's hands. The hands of you,

Dad, the hands of you. You, who held us
gently. You, who pushed us forward.
You, who let us fly.

MY PARENTS

are in love and don't try
to tell them otherwise or
they will get really angry.

ODE TO THE PERSON
WHO STOLE MY FAMILY'S LAWN GNOME
for Kev

Are you sinister?
Because I think you're sinister.

Are you evil?
Because I think you're evil.

You wait until my family is out
watching fireworks on the Fourth of July
and you up and steal my family's lawn gnome.

Did you want to register a reaction with us?
Was that your intent?

Did you watch us as we stumbled around in the dark,
wishing, hoping, praying: *Well, maybe the wind
just blew him to some other part of the lawn...*

But he was not to be found that night,
or the next morning.

He has a name.
A name my brother gave him
when we were all younger.

Did you know that?
When you pedaled furiously away,
did you whisper into his pointy elfin ears:
Hutchinson Farf, now you are mine?

Why do you need a lawn gnome?

Why do *you* need a lawn gnome?
I can tell you why we needed one.

It was used to cure my brother of his fear
of little people after he saw *The Wizard of Oz*,
and began having nightmares of being trampled
by tiny feet.

My mother purchased him from a flea market
in Lancaster and told my brother that they could
be friends. My brother was not assured.

He did not like the idea of a person much older than him,
who was the same size as his five year old self.

But it worked.

And Hutchinson Farf has had his place in our yard
for over seven years now.

Well, until you stole him, *thief.*

Until you kidnapped him, *scoundrel.*

Until you took him away and did God knows what to him,
you tiny-cocked jerk!

Why do you need a lawn gnome?

Was it for decoration?

Did you not notice that brand-spanking new
"Fat Women Bending Over" cut-out two doors down?

Or how about the perilously perched kitten clinging
to the Ganterts' garage?

Or what about the over-sized, iridescent snail
inexplicably slurping across the Napoleon's lawn
just twenty feet away, tops?

Why a lawn gnome?

Are you *fucked up* in the head?

Do you have absolutely *no* taste in lawn accouterments?

It's a fucking cement gnome!

What was the attraction?
I am very fucking curious!

My mother said I should calm down.

Maybe even *forgive* you.

That you were probably some prankster 8-year-old,
you rat bastard motherfucker.

But I can't forget.

I've grown suspicious of my neighborhood watch.

I've grown envious of my neighbor's untouched cow
placard, that reads: Crowthers' 823 Herschel Road.

So I've recounted the inventory:

Missing:	One, Hutchinson Farf
Height:	24 inches, including
	permanently stuck-on cement cap with cement bell
Eyes:	Blue
Hair:	White
Beard:	White
Last seen:	Frozen in jig position, upper center part
	of my lawn, slightly obscured by shrubbery
Owner's Heart:	Broken

I tried to lodge a complaint,
but the police just laughed.

AUGUST IN PHILADELPHIA

It is the night before I leave
for New York City and the leaves
seem to spin their last dance for me.
The branches remain crooked
and indifferent, shutting out the moon.

There's a song in Philadelphia.
It's written in sidewalk bruises, vibrates
along the soles of worn down boots.
It has a chorus of street-crack dandelions,
pretzel vendors and blue-black pigeons.

The songs run through our blood,
under our streets, I can follow it
through the sounds of water:
hard rain and ringing pipes, open
hydrants, sprinklers in the front yard
cooling round-bellied toddlers.

My last night here, and I'm lying in bed.
Down the street I hear someone singing,
the voice scratches the skyline. The skyline
scratches the sky. The bright lights
from our windows making us all look
like facets in a fat garden of jewels.

PLACES I'VE NEVER BEEN KISSED

bookstores, beaches, carnivals, funerals,
basements, weddings, family reunions,
my boyfriend's bedroom, my parent's bedroom,
malls, McDonald's, a New York City park,
in a pond, in a pool, in a prom dress,
Nevada.

SHORT LIST

If I were to name all the men I've ever kissed
it would not even fill up a post-it note,
even if you wrote in fancy, cursive script,
even if you allowed me to count 11-year-olds
as men, even if you counted closed-mouth kissing,
even if the post-it note was not a post-it note for humans,
but a post-it note created for ants that could only be
used by ants wearing business suits and spectacles,
who spent their afternoons doodling
on these post-it notes while buying and selling
stock on abandoned Doritos and that mint
I spit out onto the grass that last time
I kissed you.

DOWN THERE

This is how you refer to your genitalia.
This is also where your mother told me,
while standing at the basement door,
I could find some ice cream.

HAIKU WRITTEN IN HONOR OF YOUR BIRTHDAY

I took the subway
one stop too far, writing a
poem about you.

SIDE EFFECTS

My friend's mother is a doctor,
and she says that people like medication
that has side effects better than ones
that don't because it's proof
that the medicine is doing something.

An old boyfriend once told me
that he masturbated to me so much,
he accidentally water-proofed his hand.

Whenever you write me a letter,
I treat myself to ice cream.

CHECKLIST

People who think you should date me:
Your mother, *check.*
Your two little sisters, *check.*
All three of your brothers, *check.*
Your dad, "Invite her for dinner!" *check.*
Your friends, except for that lame-ass
money-obsessed misogynist, *check.*
You, the jury is still out,
but I think your subconscious is a *check.*
Me, *check.*
My friends,
except for the one that dated you, *check.*
Fate, *check.*
Modern science, *check.*
God, if you believed in one, *check.*

SCIENCE

When two strands of life
smash into one another and become one,
that is called fusion; cold fusion is a myth.
In order for two things to become one,
you need heat, a lot of it.

And there's always been a lot of heat
between us, Jason, whenever you get pedantic
and ramble on about science:

All your swan's neck flasks and balding
Madame Curies, all your anecdotes
about Dick Feynman's van with his own
Nobel Prize-winning Feynman's Diagrams
on the side so when people honked their horns,
rolled down their windows
and yelled:

> *Hey! Do you realize those are*
> *Feynman's Diagrams*
> *on the side of your van?*

Dick would just answer back:

> *Yes, I am Richard Feynman!*

God, I adore scientists, or maybe just you,
Jason, because you will never love me
as much as you love process.
That research, hypo,
experiment, record,
experiment, record,
experiment, record,
conclusion, thesis,
satisfaction and contempt

that is bred into you at every lab hour,
every No-Doze stoned study group,
every opportunity to dig up dinosaur bones
in Nova Scotia so that you can send me
a postcard covered in dust.

I wrote a poem about you last week
swearing up and down that I would write
    no more about you,
    no more about you,
    no more about you,
but this is not about you, Jason!
This is about science!
Your life choice! Your dream world!
And I have to write about you, Jason,
because you are my science,
because science is your God.

And no, you did not create me, and no,
you do no dictate what I do or say,
but you do control my temperatures,
you do influence my tides,
making me rise and fall and rise
    and fall and rise and fall
    and rise
according to how you see the moon.

I've had enough poets, Jason.

And I know that you get shy because
you think you don't have any metaphors,
just that old Bunsen burner you fished out
of the trash. You called it a relic and wrote
your name on it, saying you wanted to attach
yourself to a 'pre-er' science, a time
when less was known.

You are beautiful in ways you aren't even aware of.

And I'm trying to explain this all to you
over breakfast, but there is a science
to loving someone, and I have failed that course
every time I've signed up for it.

I just keep thinking about Heisenberg's Uncertainty
Principle which states that, no matter what,
there will always be something compelling our non-love,
our non-togetherness, so I'll just keep quiet and continue
eating my Florentine Omelette, if you please.

And you can talk some more about your favorite story:
Spontaneous Generation! The concept that mice came
from wheat, and flies from meat, and that smart little
Louie Pasteur proved them all wrong,
and purified milk as well.

Nothing comes from nothing! You say.

And I want to catalogue our experiences
in a white lab coat with goggles!

I want to offer up my love on a petri dish,
asking you to stain my culture
and watch it grow!

Because you are my science, Jason,
you are my endless hypothesis,
and I am tired of the
        experiment, record,
        experiment, record.
Get me to my conclusion, Jason!
Prove my thesis statement,
that states that

        you squared
        plus me squared
        equals
        love,
        squared.

And if you think this is a joke, Jason,
why don't you adapt your science
and prove me wrong.

LOVE POEM

I took a deep breath,
and told the audience
that you were in the theatre,
made a gesture, and their heads
shifted and craned to look at you.
They smiled.

Then I took another deep breath,
stepped back, and closed my eyes.
I had told the cast of the play
I was opening for, that this was
my kamikaze night: crash and burn.
I was all alone on that stage and
you were all alone in the audience.

Afterwards,
we went to dinner
at the only restaurant in New York
that you like, Chat 'n' Chew,
and I got us free dessert by singing
Happy Birthday so loudly, that
the entire restaurant was clapping
their hands by the end, and I didn't
even know the guy.

She's so special, the waitresses
told you when they crowded around
our table. One gave you a little
push on the back of your shoulder.
Do you realize that? she asked.
Yes, you said. Do you? she asked.

When they left, I smiled
at you over my coffee mug.
Magic, I said.
I said I was magic.

Later that night,
you fell asleep hours before me,
lying in my roommate's bed.
I was flat on my back, staring
at the ceiling, trying not
to think about that poem.

Sometimes words are really just words.

NIGHTFALL

I was bearing down on the night,
swinging from a maple tree
five miles from the city limits.

You were laying on the hood of your jeep,
trying to fasten your day onto something cool
and dark, your eyes exposed like comets.

I can see the city from here, I told you,
and you didn't believe me, so I pointed it
out to you when you reached the top.

We sat there for a long time, watching
the city lights filter through trees,
touching each other's arms and hands.

We were seamless and opened.

And we should have stayed there all night,
should have kept sipping at that skyline,
should've kissed until we shone like the sun.

But instead we climbed down, earthbound meteors,
tired and dirty, navigating past cicada shells.
We drove home, the stars hiding behind streetlamps.

And the moon seared quietly,
its song no match for the city.

SUBWAY POEMS

I have yet to write
a happy poem
on the subway.

Except for the one
I wrote when I discovered
that you were in love
with me.

But then, it turned out
that you were, in fact,
in love with
someone
else.

So now
that poem
is not so happy
anymore.

YESTERDAY

If it was a game,
you won.

If you wanted me to surrender,
hand me the white flag.

Uncle. Uncle. Uncle.

LAST NIGHT

My friend Amanda is house-sitting
in this really swank apartment
and she has invited all of her friends
to sleep over. Everybody is fucking
in new beds tonight, except me.
I'm reading a *National Geographic*
from 1994. The plight of the panda
was never so sad.

WHY I AVOID EYE-CONTACT

You make me happy

but you are not
a responsible enough person

to hold that kind of position
in my life.

TOO MANY: TWICE

This is the ratio of the number of poems
I've written about you to the number of times
you've called me back.

LIT
(OR TO THE SCIENTIST WHOM
I'M NOT SPEAKING TO ANYMORE)

Don't say you didn't see this coming, Jason.

Don't say you didn't realize this would be my reaction
and that you never intended for me to get all worked up,
because if that were true, then you are dumber
than Lennie from *Of Mice and Men*, blinder than Oedipus
and Tiresias put together, and can feel less
than a Dalton Trumbo character.

You put the *dick* in Dickens and the *boooo* in -kowski
and are more Coward-ly then Noël.

But you don't understand any of these references,
do you, Jason? Because you "don't read."
You are a geology major and you once told me
that, *Scientists don't read popular literature,*
Cristin, we have more important things to do.

Well, be glad you don't read, Jason,
because maybe you won't understand this
as I scream it to you on your front lawn,
on Christmas Day, brandishing
three hypodermic needles, a ginsu knife,
and a letter of permission
from Bret Easton Ellis.

Jason, you are more absurd than Ionesco.
You are more abstract than Joyce,
more inconsistent than Agatha Christie,
and more satanic than Rushdie's *Verses*.

I can't believe I used to want to Sappho you, Jason.
I used to want to Pablo Neruda you,
to Anaïs Nin and Henry Miller you. I used to want
to be O for you, to blow for you in ways
that even Odysseus' sails couldn't handle.
But self-imposed illiteracy isn't a turn-on.

You used to make fun of me being a writer,
saying: *Scientists cure diseases,*
what do writers do?

But of course, you wouldn't understand, Jason.
I mean, have you ever gotten an inner thirsting
for Zora Neale Hurston?
Or heard angels herald for you
to read F. Scott Fitzgerald?
Have you ever had a beat attack for Jack Kerouac?
The only Morrison you know is Jim, and you think
you're the noble one?

Go Plath yourself.

Your heart is so dark, even Joseph Conrad
couldn't see it, and it is so buried under bullshit
that even Poe's cops couldn't hear it.

Your mind is as empty as the libraries in *Fahrenheit 451.*
Your mind is as empty as Silas Marner's coffers.
Your mind is as empty as Huckleberry Finn's wallet.

And some people might say that this poem
is just a pretentious exercise
in seeing how many literary references
I can come up with.

And some people might complain that this poem is,
at its core, shallow, expressing the same emotion again,
and again, and again. I mean, how many times
can you articulate your contempt for Jason
before the audience gets a little bored?

But you know what, Jason? Those people
would be wrong. Because this is not the poem
I am writing to express my hatred for you.

This poem is the poem I am writing because
we aren't speaking, and it is making my heart hurt
so bad, that sometimes I can't make it up off the floor.

And this is the poem I am writing instead of writing
the *I miss having breakfast with you* poem, instead
of the *Let's walk dogs in our old schoolyard again* poem.
Instead of the *How are you doing?* poem, the *I miss you*
poem, the *I wish I was making fun of how much you like
Garth Brooks while sitting in front of your parents' house
in your jeep* poem, instead of *the Holidays are coming
around and you know what that means: SUICIDE!* poem.

I am writing this so that I can stop wanting to write
the *I could fall in love with you again so quickly
if only you would say one more word to me* poem.

But I am tired of loving you, Jason,
because you clearly don't know
how to love me right.

And if some pretentious-ass poem can stop me
from thinking about the way your laugh sounds,
about the way your skin feels in the rain,
about how I would rather be miserable with you,
than happy with anyone else in the world...

If some pretentious-ass poem can do all that?

Then I am *Gone with the Wind*, I am *On the Road*,
I am flying over that fucking cuckoo's nest,
I am gone, I am gone, I am gone.

I am.

HAIKU ABOUT LOVE AND POP CULTURE

In a frictionless world,
the mystery machine would
go on forever.

WARRANTY

We are not responsible
for any omissions or inaccuracies found here
for the validity of these postings
for any damage this may cause

We are not responsible
for anyone trying these stunts
for anyone not reading the directions fully
for anyone's beliefs besides our own

We are not responsible
for your actions
for our actions
for anything our salesmen promise or state during the sale

We are not responsible
for lost luggage
for lost messages
for damaged goods

We are not responsible
for losses that are incurred by you
for anything that may happen to you
for seagulls eating your funnel cake

We are not responsible
for any injury or damage you may have caused yourself
for any injury or damage you may be causing yourself
for any injury or damage that may occur in the future

We are not responsible
for anyone but ourselves

We are not responsible
for the whole world, you know

We are not responsible
for the past so we are not
saying we're sorry

KNOCK KNOCK POEMS

I.

Knock, knock.
> *Who's there?*
Boo.
> *Boo who?*
Crying isn't going to work any more.

II.

Knock, knock.
> *Who's there?*
True Love.
> *True Love who?*
True Love forever is great.

III.

Knock, knock.
> *Who's there?*
God.
> *God who?*
Oh, that's right. I don't exist in your modern world.

IV.

Knock, knock.
> *Who's there?*
Unborn Fetus.
> *Unborn Fetus who?*
Well, maybe if the U.S. Government respected me
as a human being then perhaps I could be given a name. [1]

---

1   *NOTE: Author is Pro-Choice, but also Pro-Hilarious-Talking-Fetus.*

V.

Knock, knock.
   Who's there?
What?
   What who?
Huh?[2]

VI.

Knock, knock.
   Who's there?
Me.
   Me who?
Why must we play these games?

---

2   *This poem is infinitely funnier for the person initiating the poem than it is for the person hearing it.*

HARD BARGAIN

I am auctioning off my virginity
to the highest bidder.

I am not—and let me make
this perfectly clear—I am not
being metaphorical here.

I want cold hard cash
for my tight hot ethics.

I am sick of my virginity.

Back in the day, when we were eight, shit,
everyone was saving themselves for marriage,
or at least college, or at least a stable relationship,
but now I've got friends' little sisters giving me
advice on hand jobs,

and I don't have to put up with this crap,
because I'm in college and if there is one thing
I've learned about virginity in college,
it is that it is, at best, an anecdote,
and not having a good anecdote is one thing,
but the reactions are a whole other story.

All the girls with their:

> *Well, don't worry.*
> *You're bound to find someone.*

And all the guys, and sometimes
these are guys that I am interested in,
all the guys with their:

> *Oh.*
> *Well, that explains a lot.*

I don't need to be putting up with this shit.

I am turning twenty in 149 days, and if there is
one thing that I have learned about virginity
anecdotes, it is that when you turn twenty,
the stories go from charming and poignant
to depressing and pathetic.

So that's when it came to me: *Prostitution*!

What a great foray into the sexual experience!
And let's be honest: what a great anecdote.

My plan, at first, was to sell everything that I have
of merit, buy a round trip ticket to San Francisco,
rent a car, and even though I don't drive, drive that car
down the darkest, poorest, scariest alley in all of San Fran—
the one that I read about in those Covenant House pamphlets
my mom would get from the Jehovah's Witnesses—
and find the youngest, most heroin-addicted,
wild-eyed, fresh-faced prostitute, and open up
my car door and flash 200 crisp one dollar bills
and say,

> *Get in.*

And I wouldn't tell him I'm a virgin.
I would tell him I'm a nympho, and I would take
him to a fancy hotel, and clean him up,
and lie him on silk sheets, and fuck him
like I've never fucked before, because I haven't
ever fucked before.

But then, just as this fantasy gets good, I remember:
syphilis, gonorrhea, hepatitis A, B, C, the clap,
body lice, genital warts, crabs, scabies, chlamydia,
and AIDS.

And then it hit me.

Sell... *myself?*

Fucking brilliant.

Fuck, I would be this thing,
this whole underground sex world thing.
Businessmen from Tokyo would be calling
businessmen on Wall Street, who would be
calling up Heidi Fleiss in prison asking:
How do I get a piece of that?

Rich kids from LA would be logging on to
www.hymen.com for hourly updates.

Entire Italian villages would pool their money
so that I could lose it with the town schlong:
Ernesto, with the enormous cock that smells
suspiciously like flan and is crooked to the left.

I could get corporate sponsors:

> *This defloweration is brought to you
> by Ivory Soap, 99.9% pure!*

I could sell the rights to HBO.

I would have to shave my pubic hair
into the Nike Swoosh logo.

And after it is all over, and the hype dies down,
I'll sit in my new 36th floor apartment on my sofa
made of twenties, and I'll make myself some tea,
pull down the curtains, turn off the lights, close
my eyes, and lie in the dark of the room,
trying to remember
what it was like
to be

a virgin.

But until then,
let the bidding begin.

THE GUY WHO HATED MY STUFF ON POEMFONE[3] (A FOUND POEM)

With patience,
I have heard your poetry
like every single other piece of crap
that I have heard on PoemFone
for as far back as I can remember
when Penny Cade? Penny Arcade?
Came on in 95 and 96?

I really do not understand
what it is you people call poetry.

I mean, I honestly don't understand
what it is that you call poetry, this crap.
I mean, do you?

Are you honestly proud of what you write?

Do you honestly sit down,
aware of what you are doing,
and with full comprehension
of what it is that you are doing,
say to people, let alone *strangers*,
that this is what you write?

If it's friends, maybe, out of pity,
they might say: Yes, your work is all right.

---

3   Poemfone was an NYC-based arts project, where people could call in and
listen to a new poem every day via voice message service. A different poet was selected
to participate each month, and this poem is an exact transcription of an anonymous
voicemail message which had been left in response to one of my poems during my
Poemfone month.

But a stranger?

I mean, it is just nonsense.

I honestly don't know what it is
you people do with your lives,
what it is you really do,
what your profession is,
but I hope, God, I hope
you don't expect, in any way,
shape, or form, to be remembered
for what it is you write.

I don't say this as a hard person
putting down another person,
because if I wrote something
and it was shit, I would expect
people to tell me it was garbage,
that way I could improve,
I could understand what it is
that I was lacking.

And not from one person,
as many people as I could
possibly get an opinion from,
to see if my work is
at all worthwhile reading.

But your stuff is crap.
Genuine gar-*bage*.

And this might just be me,
I mean, maybe I am the only one
who views your stuff as crap.

Maybe I'm the only one that calls once
in a while with curiosity to see
if anything has improved
in this poemfone.

I mean, maybe it's just me.
So, it's just one person,
but your stuff is *crap*.

BROKENDOWNMACHINE

1.
INBREEDING
I am very much against inbreeding.
Except when you say that
you love me like a sister.

2.
THE PLAN
I'll just keep being
really smart and pretty
until you realize it
and fall in love with me.

3.
OVERCOMPENSATING
This is what I feel people are doing
when I see them pawing each other
in public.

They are just overcompensating,
I think, for the fact that they can't
have me.

4.
I AM SMARTER THAN HER
and that is my only consolation.

5.
OPTIMIST
Steven,
that guy from the depression hotline,
sounded really cute.

NOTES FROM THE HOTEL SUZÇOUF

Last night, the couple next door was at it again.
He spoke German like a man off a language cassette
and she giggled sweetly, loudly. Lovemaking sounds
so different here, like time doesn't exist, like this isn't
a cheap hotel, like I am not listening, crouched tight
in my bed. Kim says we got the rooms cheap because
the owner thinks we are lesbians. He speaks a soft
and beautiful English. His cheeks are red. *Good Year,*
Happy Year, he said, greeting us with our keys
as we stumbled in late New Year's morning.

We were tired and beaten. Festivals on the Champs-Elsyée
left us dodging bottle rockets and the plump wet meat of lips.
Bonne Année, they would slur, wrapping their fingers
around our thighs and necks. We couldn't even see the metro.
Later we sat in our quiet room, slumped over butter cookies
and juice that we lifted from a marché in Pigalle.

Maybe it's a custom, Kim said, shrugging off the images
of the night: the strange optimism, the ecstasy, the promise
of new things, the sick flattery of hands, the strain of eyes.

The couple next door moved in two days later.
Kim says the man looks cruel, and I worry when the sex
becomes too hard, when the grunts become overly male
and the armoire bangs anxiously against the wall. Kim hears
nothing of this. She sleeps well and deeply. She only knows
the quick Swedes next door who flick up the stairs
with tiny leather-framed legs, then spend the afternoon
smoking up and listening to the Stones and the Doors.

Our hotel is tiny and the windows open up to an apartment
complex. On New Year's, we hung out them and wished
Bonne Année to the lingering French who smoked on their balconies.

They raised their wine bottles, unfazed. I wonder if they know
we look into their windows—Kim and I both in the afternoon, and
me, alone, into the night. I wonder if they realize what I have seen:
all the early morning lovemaking on counters, the nights spent alone
in kitchens, the angry telephones whirled in the air. They don't
appear to, they lift their bottles fearlessly, *Bonne Année.*

Kim is asleep now. We went to Versailles in the morning
and we wilted like flowers when it rained. Our hotel room is warm
(and quiet, the Germans and Swedes are loose in the city). We joked
about the concierge, his limp smile and soft voice and then she slipped
between the covers while I kept watch. She says it is forbidden for me
to sleep during the day: *Interdit!* She says it will keep me up nights
and it's true.

Kim falls asleep so quickly. I sit in a stiff backed chair eating
what's left of the bread we bought for tomorrow's breakfast. I watch Kim,
all damp curl and open mouth. I understand why the concierge thinks
we are lovers: she is very beautiful. Outside, the Paris rain has stopped
and the sky is clear. It's time for dinner, but I'll let Kim sleep.

If someone asked me, I would say the Germans are at Sacré-Cœur,
the Sacred Heart, trying to find ecstasy between the old stone walls
and the cityscape that took centuries to build. I would say that
the Swedes were at Père Lachaise; the male Swede says that
they visit Jim's grave everyday. I picture them tomb-side, thankful
that the rain has stopped so that they can do another etching before the guard
stops them: *James Douglas Morrison* and a date they can never get right.

And I would say I would be here, rubbing tired eyes
and cursing my body for its maladjustment, slouching forehead
against window. And that Kim would be here, too, asleep, and
that Paris would be where it is: behind my window
and over the balcony, pressed into the streets like a scrapbook,
the Seine sleeping soundly in its own bed.

We would all sigh deeply.

The rain has stopped and there is so little to do.

EUROPE

When I went to Paris,
I collected one pebble
for every time I thought
of you.

I was going to present them to you
upon my return; my love for you,
for once, was going to be something
tangible: a big rattling bottle of thought.

But I lost my nerve at the last minute.
I mean, of course I did. So instead,
I scattered the French pebbles
with the stones on your driveway.

And now I feel so stupid,
treading on top of their meaning
as I find my way to your porch
for yet another platonic breakfast.

I LOVE YOU

the last time you
said this to me
we were still
in high school.

I never said it
to you.

And although
I wish
it were different,

we will probably
never say it
to each other again.

Which is why
you will never
read this book.

THE WORST ANNIVERSARY GIFT I EVER GOT

A 25% off coupon
for a discount bra store
at the largest outlet mall
in Pennsylvania.

THE WORST VALENTINE'S GIFT I EVER GOT

We had been dating for three months,
and he got me a mug which read:

Friends are people who never let you forget
all the stupid things you've done.

RYAN

Of all the names that can be given to a boy,
Ryan was the name that the gods destined
I would develop the most crushes on.

I guess they figured this because I was a poet,
and, you know:

Ryan
Crying

SOMERTON STATION

is the train station
near my house

where nothing
romantic
ever happened
to me.

Mostly just
sad things.

Mostly just
things that never
worked out.

Because nothing
ever works out
for me.

Because nobody
loves me and
I love nobody.

Writing this poem
is making me
sad.

PROMS

I went to 8 proms in high school.

Although I would later change my mind,
I never liked my dates enough
to live out any of the prom night clichés:

kissing during the last song;
the hotel room afterwards;
perhaps the loosening of virginities,
if not the loss of them altogether;
being in love forever.

I kept all the corsages, still drying
on the hooks in my closet.

Some nights I try one on.
Some nights, two. Some, three.

And some lonely long summer nights,
I try on all eight, imagining all the dates
converging suddenly in my bedroom,
thinking me beautiful in pjs and flowers.

ROADTRIP, FRONT SEAT, TENNESSEE, 2:57AM

I suck on an orange fruit ball.

This is what I imagine your mouth
tastes like on long car trips,
because coffee makes you jumpy
and you don't like soda.

America is the most beautiful
when seen from the highway at 3am.
There is a gentleness shared among
the drivers at night.

There is no ego on a highway at 3am.
Only concepts of destination
and soft orange fruit balls.

I want to kiss you, but instead I push
another piece of candy past my lips.

Outside, the highway stretches in front of us
like the opposite of a metaphor,
like the flipside of our flesh,
like extensions of our dull nerves,
like a dry tongue.

HARRISBURG

This is number one, and it's open to the first page.

Already, I wish that if something had to be let go,
it would've been all the other letters, the ones we kept
in empty cups, weighted at the bottom of our bags,
stuffed under our dorm room sinks.

Turn the page, and begin to read aloud

to the summer fan just knocking about hot air,
pens spilling out of mugs, a cardboard mailing box
still stiff in all this wet summer. I sit on the edge
of my bed, forever in love with the wrong boy

and this is
where the stars come in (on page seventeen)

and you wrote me about the birth of radio,
and your dreams of snow falling on water,
and how the night was always pushing
across the brown factory sky. I now know:
I should have loved you more.
I should have loved you better.

And somewhere, somebody turned a switch

and my city woke up without you.
Tonight you curl around a woman
I've never met and I sleepwalk into this.
It's just, I wanted to let you know you
could've had anything, anything,
and that you should have had more.

HAIKU FOR PETER

Like the crisp white moon
reflecting the light of the
sun, am I to you.

DEATH FARM

Everyone knew Andy's brother, Mike, worked at the Death Farm, though no one knew exactly what he did.

All anybody could really say, was that Mike left at 6 in the morning and returned 12 hours later, looking pretty much the same.

Andy thought I deserved to know this about his brother, Mike, considering that I was visiting for the weekend from Philadelphia, and he wanted to assure me that Mike was a good guy, and that he would never harm anyone, and that a job's a job.

When I told him I didn't know what the Death Farm was, Andy nearly drove off the road.

Every city and every town has their stories.

In my neighborhood in Philadelphia, we'd stay up late and go to some shit-filled pond where some kid was supposed to have drowned years ago and they never found the body. We'd scare ourselves hoarse, screaming that we could see him under the water, see his hands reaching up at us. This is how a lot of us got our first kiss: screaming and reaching towards the one person we wanted to make us feel safe.

In Port Royal, in Central Pennsylvania, where Andy's from, there was the Death Farm, which wasn't so much a ghost story and certainly wasn't romantic.

The story goes, Andy told me, that sometime in the 60's or the 70's, the US government bought up the Trainer family's huge orchard and let the place go wild. Then, they built the facility deep in the land so no one could see, and kept it all hush hush what they were doing.

But somehow it got out that the 175-acres of what used to be an orchard were now littered with bodies, bodies that were donated to science, bodies that the FBI would then cut, stab, shoot, submerge under water for days, carve letters into, tie up with ropes, run over with cars, and do whatever else the crazy people of the world would do to another human being at the time, and then the bodies would be placed all over what used to be an orchard. Then trainees or FBI investigators would go out and find them, study the effects on the bodies, create theories about the mind of the killer, try to understand what happened and why.

The first time I heard about it, I thought Andy was joshing me. He offered to drive by it, but I wouldn't let him.

Eventually we did, late at night on Sunday, and the place was packed, irresistible to teenagers. Everyone got out of their cars, and walked alongside the high, electric fence, putting face to metal and peering into the brush, claiming to see a hand or a foot sticking out of a drainage pipe or floating in the shallow creek. But no one could actually prove a thing. It was kind of funny in a sick way.

People kept asking Andy about what his brother did, first to get his goat, but then out of sincere curiosity, and he answered them, the way he answered me: with the truth.

Mike never told anyone what he did. He wasn't allowed.

I didn't get to meet Mike, until Sunday, when Andy got sick and Andy's mom got Mike to drive me the hour's drive to the train station. We kept quiet for most of the ride. The radio was broken, so Mike had a boom box, and we listened to a mix tape he had made of heavy metal and hard rock, mostly:

> *I love Rock 'n' Roll!*
> *Put another dime*
> *in the jukebox, baby!*

But night was closing in, and the hour's drive seemed to be taking three times that amount.

It would be a lie to say I didn't feel scared, that I didn't want to jump out of the car, though I really knew nothing about Andy's brother. It would be a lie to say that I didn't suddenly believe what I had been hearing from all of Andy's friends, that Mike was the guy in charge of screwing around with the bodies, and this is how he got his rocks off. I mean, I knew it was bullshit, but I couldn't say at age 16, all alone in that car, that I wasn't scared.

The radio was broken. The street was so dark.

Then, after about 45 minutes into the trip, Mike spoke.

You know, I read this real interesting thing yesterday, he began, clearing his throat, *I read that babies remember what it's like to be in the womb up until the age of 2 or 3. That if you ask them what it's like, they say, something like, oh you know, it was warm, and it was really dark and wet.*

Isn't that amazing, he said.

Yeah, I replied.

We smiled at each other. Simple.

He let me out at the train station and I thanked him.

I never talked to Mike again, and never went back to Port Royal, and the last time I really talked to Andy was when he took my friend to her senior prom.

But last spring, I was at Bard, and I bumped into him. I asked him about his life, and Port Royal. He said that the Death Farm is still open, but that Mike has quit.

He works at Hershey now, he said, *he's in charge of the kisses.*

FOR PHIL,
ON THE OCCASION OF HIS 21ˢᵀ BIRTHDAY

Summertime, and we couldn't raise our voices
high enough. 21, and you breathed warm air.
You with your wine-colored cheeks:
I could do nothing but blush.

High enough? 21, and you breathed warm air,
and all I could do was taste the sweat of your words.
I could do nothing but blush.
Lauren and Erin were slick with kisses,

and all I could do was taste the sweat of your words.
I arched my body forward and we laughed, breathed.
Lauren and Erin were slick with kisses.
21, and you were the most beautiful creature I'd seen.

I arched my body forward and we laughed, breathed.
All I wanted to do was write poetry about this:
21, and you were the most beautiful creature I'd seen.
We sunk into each other's skin on the couch.

All I wanted to do was write poetry about this
night: you and me and the world, dancing.
We sunk into each other's skin. On the couch
I could have laughed all

night: you and me and the world, dancing.
We swung our bodies until they were one.
I could have laughed all
summer: it was almost over.

We swung our bodies until they were one.
Tired, we leaned into each other to get home.
Summer: it was almost over.
If I could take any of this back...

Tired, we leaned into each other to get home.
Summertime and we couldn't raise our voices.
If I could take any of this back:
you and your wine-colored cheeks.

TO THE BOY WHO BUILDS AND PAINTS SETS AT THE ARDEN THEATRE COMPANY IN PHILADELPHIA

Oh, Boy Who Builds and Paints Sets
at the Arden Theatre Company in Philadelphia!
It is to you that I raise my sneakers—
the ones that you stained when you accidently
spilled paint on them: Parillo Red 158,
the color of my cheeks after you kept apologizing
and apologizing and apologizing.

Oh, Boy Who Builds and Paints Sets
at the Arden Theatre Company in Philadelphia!
It is to you that I raise my humus and tofu sandwich—
the one that I've bought every day since you told me
about the restaurant, hands on hips, tool belt slouching,
extolling the virtues of protein in a vegetarian's diet.

Oh, Boy Who Builds and Paints Sets
at the Arden Theatre Company in Philadelphia!
It is to you that I raise my eyes, my eyebrows,
my expectations, but not my head, as I walk swiftly
and suspiciously past the stage again, hoping that you
will call out my name so that I can answer back:
Yes, Perry!

Who was your mother, Perry, so that I can thank her.
Did she have paint-stained hands as well? Will your
children? Will the neo-natal nurses get red-faced
scrubbing your infant's tiny flecked fingers
with lava soap and a bristle brush?

Will you build your children dramatic cradles
and paint them with non-toxic inks?

I fantasize about you working constantly,
and not just building sets, but your old jobs
as well, using information that I gleaned
from the only true conversation we've ever had,
that time in the green room backstage when you
ate M&M's and drank Yoo-Hoo.

The images of a past you roll around in my head:

The you that worked at the health food store!
The you that worked at the florist!
The you that worked as a chocolate inspector
at a factory in Hershey!

You said that they fired you because you ate too much candy.
Are you stealing from here as well? Are you building sets in
your backyard, and praying for actors to come?

If I had the money, I would buy you all the loose and loopy
corduroys that your armoires could hold. I would raid
Salvation Armies for those grade school tee-shirts
that hug your long and narrow columns of tight ribs
and flesh. I would buy you even more of those glasses
that are too big for your face, so that you can look sloppy
and curious, pushing the frames up with the one finger
you keep paint free.

I would flood your bathroom with Lava soap.

But alas, oh, Boy Who Builds and Paints
Sets at the Arden Theatre Company in Philadelphia!
Oh, Boy Who the Gods and the Angels and the Interns
and the Actors and your Mother call Perry! You do not
care for the playwright upstairs nor for the secretaries
who click their tongues at the paint you spill in the
stairwell. Nor for the silly actresses who giggle
and gossip that you're gay.

Nor do you care for this stuttering girl
with her paint-stained shoes who shyly watches you
from the mezzanine, pressing herself up against the wall,
feeling her own small heat.

You only care about the set and the paint
and the play which has not even been cast yet
but for which you have already built the world.

EX-BOYFRIEND

When I went to the WaWa
to see if my ex-boyfriend still worked there,
I discovered it had been turned
into a funeral home.

Now how am I supposed to kill him?

I think it takes me longer than most
to get over my ex-boyfriends.

Or rather, ex-boy*friend*,
for there is only one,
only one who counts.

The one, the He,
who dumped me
for that trampy, white-trash,
I-want-to-get-with-you-at-a-dairy-queen,
ill-mannered, submissive, giggling,
tight-jeaned, loose-kneed,
porn-for-the-patriarchy poster girl:
Marissa.

Marissa, whom he met
at a bowling alley.

My friends tell me
that I need to stop harping
on him, and just move on.

Fuck you.

See, I have some sort of emotional problem
that prevents me from getting in touch
with my anger, except for one situation,
the one, the He, the ex-boyfriend.

I worship my ex-boyfriend
like a bad star.

I cannot tell you his name
because I cannot be positive
that you are not his friend
that he has sent to spy on me
because he is secretly in love
with me but afraid that I'll find out.

If you are my ex-boyfriend,
then you are reading this by accident.

If you are my ex-boyfriend,
then inside your chest
beats a heart made of
deformed stuffed animals.

Symbolism.

I never loved you.
I keep your hair in envelopes in my closet.
I am the one who has your Klimt book.

Only one of these things is true.

EX-BOYFRIEND!

When will you die
so that I can start writing
good ex-boyfriend poetry
which really is
dead ex-boyfriend poetry,

free from all the requisite
living ex-boyfriend bitterness.

The last time I went on a date
with someone new, I chewed
all the leather off my sleeves
waiting for him to choose
a song at the jukebox.

I am not made
to date someone new.

EX-BOYFRIEND!

Your cologne is everywhere.

EX-BOYFRIEND!

I have a mug with your name on it!

EX-BOYFRIEND!

I want to kill you with gasoline
and cheesecake!

I want to kill you with gasoline
and comic books!

I want to kill you with gasoline
and prom pictures!

EX-BOYFRIEND!

How long do I have to lay on this floor
before you fall in love with me again?

ON WHY I HATE THE OCEAN

I hate the ocean. I hate that fucking ocean.
Who doesn't? Who doesn't hate the ocean?
Well, you. You don't hate the ocean.
But I do.

I hate the ocean because it's filled with jellyfish
and stinging nettles and giant sharks and garbage
and medical waste and pirate ships and the Titanic.

I hate that it's filled with sand that gets caught
in my bathing suit and all that rank, lung-filling seawater
and stupid waves that knock me over, again and again
and again. And I hate how you have to keep walking back
to your dumb little umbrella again and again and again,
because the tide keeps sweeping you away, just keeps
sweeping you away, right down the beach, and away
from where you belong, and then you've got to get out
and walk back, walk back down the beach, past
all these strange, ugly, naked people,
and I hate it.

And the ocean?

The ocean just laughs.
Just laughs and laughs and laughs.
Fucking ocean.

But most of all, I hate the ocean
because you once told me that I couldn't.

You said that I couldn't possibly hate the ocean,
that one simply cannot hate something so large,
so deep, or so complex. That it was impossible.
That I was probably just being naïve or reactionary.
That I probably just wasn't really thinking it through,
overly emotional me, not being serious again.

And there was truth to your statement:
I didn't really hate the ocean.

I mean I don't hate it the way I hate homophobes.
It's not like I want the ocean dead.
I am not asking for someone to kill the ocean.

I know the ocean has merit:
I mean, rain for one. Dolphins, being another.

But I do strongly dislike the ocean,
and was only saying that I hated it
to make you laugh... which you didn't.
And I hated that you saw through it,
and instead of finding me charming,
you found me tedious,
a fate even worse than unfunny.

You probably don't remember this discussion.
Nor should you have, really, since it is not
the role of the crush to remember.
The crush simply exists.
It is the role of the crushed to record.

You don't remember that conversation,
but I do. I carry it around with me 24/7.
It jangles like piles of sea glass.

It's stupid how much I can remember,
and even dumber that if I didn't hate the ocean
then, I certainly do now, along with every other
thing that reminds me of you:

breakfasts and jeeps and forever backyard barbeques
and happy meals and old movie theatres and the moment
on busy roads in the early, early morning when the traffic
breaks all around you, and it looks like no one is there,
just you and the person you are with,
and then sometimes,
just you.

I hate all these things, and I shouldn't.
I should hate you, but I don't.
I just need to move on, but I am stuck.
But I think I'm beginning to understand.

This morning, the clouds outside my window
burst into tears the moment I woke up,
and I finally heard what they were saying:

You can only hold on to things for so long.
Sometimes you've just got to let go.

CHROME GRAVITY

We woke up before the sun
every Saturday morning in September,
making sure we were brushed and presentable
by eight at the latest, and met on his porch
before the day could even say the word, *Love*.

By October, we were meeting at six.
He'd be sleepy-eyed and grinning, still unfocused
and crooked on the couch when I knocked.
His parents would be asleep so we would creep
around the house trying to find his shoes and a hat
before we hit the gravel and walked half a mile
to Suburban House Diner, the best in the world,
and only three city blocks in from Bucks County.

We found our table in mid-November.
It was made of plastic and glitter,
didn't have one cigarette burn,
was close to the jukebox and the bathroom,
and the only booth in the whole joint
that had a number: thirty-eight.
We christened it with coffee spills.

We watched traffic and people,
and ordered a different omelet every week
in December. We even saw Santa eating
chipped beef on Christmas Eve, complaining
about business and giving all the waitresses
candy canes and reindeer made of pipe cleaners.

We found romance swimming in pineapple juice
one bleary-eyed January morning, when the frost
had just begun to creep into the sidewalk cracks
and we were just kids from the other side of County Line,
holding hands under the table, rushing our meals
to get back home.

In February, they took the jukebox out for repairs,
and said they weren't sure if it was coming back.
It was expensive to fix and didn't really bring
in a lot of money. We frowned over our pancakes
and over-priced waffles. Valentine's Day was silent
and white, snow falling like ribbon, spreading
thin its welcome, the truck drivers cursing.

He called last night,
and it was the first time I'd heard his voice
since March when we finished our breakfasts in silence
and walked home in different directions,
stiffing the waitress and adding a new chill
to the crisp spring air.

He spoke about the magic of the diner,
and how they had just redone the interior for Easter,
how they had added a new omelet of the month,
some sacrilege creation in the form of a cross.
They even installed a new jukebox.

It plays all the old stuff, he said,
it plays all the old stuff like memories.

YES

I woke up this morning
and thought of you while
I was brushing my teeth.

I smiled.

That's the poem right there.

ACKNOWLEDGEMENTS

Grateful acknowledgements are made to the following journals in which some of these writings first appeared in slightly different forms:

The Legendary – "Warranty"
The Waverly Review – "Lit; Or to the Scientist Whom I'm Not Speaking to Anymore"
Voiceworks: The Australian Youth Quarterly – "Lit; Or to the Scientist Whom I'm Not Speaking to Anymore"

Additionally, grateful acknowledgements are made to the following print and audio anthologies, in which some of the following poems have also appeared:

My Love in a Petri Dish (Kapow! 2001) – "Down There," "To The Boy Who Builds and Paints Sets at the Arden Theatre Company in Philadelphia," Side Effects" and "Science"
Poetry Slam: The Competitive Art of Performance Poetry (Manic D Press, 2001) – "Hard Bargain"
Will Work for Peace: New Political Poems – "Hard Bargain"
Word Warriors: 35 Women Leaders in the Spoken Word Revolution (Seal Press, 2007) – "Lit; Or to the Scientist Whom I'm Not Speaking to Anymore"
Going Down Swinging #30 (CD) – "Warranty"
nycSLAMS (CD) – "Mother"
Indiefeed Performance Poetry Podcast (performancepoetry.indiefeed.com) – "Mother" and "Lit; Or to the Scientist Whom I'm Not Speaking to Anymore"

Lastly, grateful acknowledgements are made to **Steve Marsh** and **The Wordsmith Press**, who published an earlier edition of this book.

ABOUT THE AUTHOR

CRISTIN O'KEEFE APTOWICZ is the author of four other books of poetry: *Hot Teen Slut, Oh, Terrible Youth, Working Class Represent*, and *Everything is Everything*. She is also the author of the non-fiction book, *Words In Your Face: A Guided Tour Through Twenty Years of the New York City Poetry Slam*, which *The Washington Post* named as one of five Notable Books on Exploring Poetry in 2008. Born and raised in Philadelphia, Aptowicz moved to New York City at the age of 17. At age 19, she founded the three-time National Poetry Slam championship poetry series NYC-Urbana, which is still held weekly at the NYC's famed Bowery Poetry Club. Most recently, Aptowicz was named the 2010-2011 ArtsEdge Writer-In-Residence at the University of Pennsylvania and was also awarded a 2011 National Endowment for the Arts Fellowship in Poetry.

For more information, please visit her website:
www.aptowicz.com.

NEW WRITE BLOODY BOOKS FOR 2011

DEAR FUTURE BOYFRIEND
A Write Bloody reissue of Cristin O'Keefe Aptowicz's first book of poetry

HOT TEEN SLUT
A Write Bloody reissue of Cristin O'Keefe Aptowicz's second book of poetry
about her time writing for porn

WORKING CLASS REPRESENT
A Write Bloody reissue of Cristin O'Keefe Aptowicz's third book of poetry

OH, TERRIBLE YOUTH
A Write Bloody reissue of Cristin O'Keefe Aptowicz's fourth book of poetry
about her terrible youth

38 BAR BLUES
A collection of poems by C.R .Avery

WORKIN' MIME TO FIVE
Humor by Derrick Brown

REASONS TO LEAVE THE SLAUGHTER
New poems by Ben Clark

YESTERDAY WON'T GOODBYE
New poems by Brian Ellis

WRITE ABOUT AN EMPTY BIRDCAGE
New poems by Elaina M. Ellis

THESE ARE THE BREAKS
New prose by Idris Goodwin

BRING DOWN THE CHANDELIERS
New poems by Tara Hardy

THE FEATHER ROOM
New poems by Anis Mojgani

LOVE IN A TIME OF ROBOT APOCALYPSE
New poems by David Perez

THE NEW CLEAN
New poems by Jon Sands

THE UNDISPUTED GREATEST WRITER OF ALL TIME
New poems by Beau Sia

SUNSET AT THE TEMPLE OF OLIVES
New poems by Paul Suntup

GENTLEMAN PRACTICE
New poems by Buddy Wakefield

HOW TO SEDUCE A WHITE BOY IN TEN EASY STEPS
New poems by Laura Yes Yes

OTHER WRITE BLOODY BOOKS (2003 - 2010)

STEVE ABEE, GREAT BALLS OF FLOWERS (2009)
New poems by Steve Abee

EVERYTHING IS EVERYTHING (2010)
New poems by Cristin O'Keefe Aptowicz

CATACOMB CONFETTI (2010)
New poems by Josh Boyd

BORN IN THE YEAR OF THE BUTTERFLY KNIFE (2004)
Poetry collection, 1994-2004 by Derrick Brown

I LOVE YOU IS BACK (2006)
Poetry compilation (2004-2006) by Derrick Brown

SCANDALABRA (2009)
New poetry compilation by Derrick Brown

DON'T SMELL THE FLOSS (2009)
New Short Fiction Pieces By Matty Byloos

THE BONES BELOW (2010)
New poems by Sierra DeMulder

THE CONSTANT VELOCITY OF TRAINS (2008)
New poems by Lea C. Deschenes

HEAVY LEAD BIRDSONG (2008)
New poems by Ryler Dustin

WRITE BLOODY ANTHOLOGIES

THE ELEPHANT ENGINE HIGH DIVE REVIVAL (2009)
Poetry by Buddy Wakefield, Derrick Brown,
Anis Mojgani, Shira Erlichman and many more!

THE GOOD THINGS ABOUT AMERICA (2009)
An illustrated, un-cynical look at our American Landscape. Various authors.
Edited by Kevin Staniec and Derrick Brown

JUNKYARD GHOST REVIVAL (2008)
Poetry by Andrea Gibson, Buddy Wakefield, Anis Mojgani,
Derrick Brown, Robbie Q, Sonya Renee and Cristin O'Keefe Aptowicz

THE LAST AMERICAN VALENTINE:
ILLUSTRATED POEMS TO SEDUCE AND DESTROY (2008)
24 authors, 12 illustrators team up for a collection of non-sappy love poetry.
Edited by Derrick Brown

LEARN THEN BURN (2010)
Anthology of poems for the classroom. Edited by Tim Stafford and Derrick Brown.

LEARN THEN BURN TEACHER'S MANUAL (2010)
Companion volume to the *Learn Then Burn* anthology. Includes lesson plans and worksheets for educators.
Edited by Tim Stafford and Molly Meacham.

WRITEBLOODY
QUALITY AMERICAN BOOKS

WWW.WRITEBLOODY.COM

WRITEBLOODY
QUALITY AMERICAN BOOKS

PULL YOUR BOOKS UP BY THEIR BOOTSTRAPS

Write Bloody Publishing distributes and promotes great books of fiction, poetry and art every year. We are an independent press dedicated to quality literature and book design, with an office in Long Beach, CA.

Our employees are authors and artists so we call ourselves a family. Our design team comes from all over America: modern painters, photographers and rock album designers create book covers we're proud to be judged by.

We publish and promote 8-12 tour-savvy authors per year. We are grass-roots, D.I.Y., bootstrap believers. Pull up a good book and join the family. Support independent authors, artists and presses.

Visit us online:
WRITEBLOODY.COM

Lightning Source UK Ltd.
Milton Keynes UK
UKHW040647221119
354046UK00003B/592/P